*In memory of the fallen from North Petherton.*

*With thanks to the Year 6 children at North Petherton Community Primary School (2022/23) for their help with this project.*

FIRST PUBLISHED 2023
CITYSCAPE PUBLISHING
ISBN: 978-1-9164164-7-5

TEXT COPYRIGHT © ANDREW POWELL-THOMAS, 2023

FRONT COVER CLOCKWISE FROM TOP LEFT: F C BANES WALKER; NORTH PETHERTON WAR MEMORIAL ST MARY'S CHURCH; STANLEY POCOCK; GRAVE OF S. J. CROCKER GWALIA CEMETERY, BELGIUM.
BACK COVER: UNVEILING OF THE WAR MEMORIAL AT CONGREGATIONAL SUNDAY SCHOOL 1923.

# NORTH PETHERTON

# REMEMBERS

ANDREW POWELL-THOMAS

ISBN: 978-1-9164164-7-5

# CONTENTS

# NORTH PETHERTON WAR MEMORIAL

In the years that followed the First World War, the biggest ever wave of public commemoration saw tens of thousands of memorials erected right across the commonwealth, and the town of North Petherton in Somerset was no different. Numerous men had left their quiet life in the country to fight on battlefields right across the world, from the trenches of Flanders to the deserts in Egypt, with some never to return.

The joy and celebration of Armistice in 1918 was understandably darkened for many with the sense of loss they had suffered - the town had lost 'some of their own' and everyone knew someone who had grieved.

Memorials to the fallen were designed and created as a necessary act of remembrance right across the country, but constructing them was often a fraught process. Parish councils had little money themselves to go towards building them, and they relied on donations and fundraising from the local community to raise the necessary amount. It is not surprising that those who had lost loved ones felt more of a burden to contribute, and if a community was fortunate, a wealthy local benefactor may have been able to provide significant backing to the building costs.

Opinions often differed as to the best form and location for a war memorial and there is no reason to believe the community of North Petherton were any different - keeping everyone appeased was a delicate process.

The town unveiled the war memorial on 1 February 1923 at the Congregational Sunday School.

# NORTH PETHERTON WAR MEMORIAL

Installed into its current location at St Mary's Church, the memorial is a wall-mounted bronze plaque with a wooden surround.

The 41 names from the First World War are listed alphabetically in raised lettering across three columns. The middle column contains a cross and the inscription:

*"To the glory of God and in memory of the men of North Petherton who gave their lives for their country in the great war"*

A little over twenty years later the Second World War began, and the 14 names of those lost from the town were added in a separate plaque, designed in a similar style to that of the first.

Today, they stand together as a testament to the bravery of those who paid the ultimate price in the fight for freedom.

Lest we forget.

# JAMES ADAMS

**Service Number:** 309198
**Rank:** Petty Officer Stoker
      HMS Valkyrie
**Born:** 3 June 1883
**Died:** 22 December 1917
**Buried:** Wembdon Road Cemetery
      Bridgwater, Somerset

James Adams was born on 3 June 1883 in the village of Thurloxten. By the time he was 7 years old his parents, Robert and Eliza, had moved the family to Huntworth, which was within the parish of North Petherton.

After leaving school he initially became a brickyard labourer and then at the age of 22, he joined the navy on 13 November 1905 and served on a number of ships before the Great War began. In 1911 he married Eliza and they lived at 4 Halesleigh Road in Bridgwater - which explains why he is buried at Wembdon Road Cemetery and not in North Petherton.

James began the conflict on board *HMS Cornwall*, before serving on the newly completed *HMS Valkyrie* in June 1917.

On 22 December 1917, the ship was part of the escort for a convoy to the Netherlands when she struck a mine. 19 men lost their lives - James being one.

*HMS Valkyrie*

# SIDNEY AISH

**Service Number:** R/1197
**Rank:** Able Seaman
       Drake Battalion. R.N.D
**Born:** 13 February 1897
**Died:** 31 October 1917
**Buried:** New Irish Farm Cemetery
         St Jean-les-Ypres, Belgium

Sidney Charles Aish was born on 13 February 1897 to James and Eliza Aish of High Street, North Petherton. One of eight children, at the age of fourteen he was earning some extra money for the family as an errand boy.

Sidney joined the Army Reserve on 9 December 1915, before entering the Royal Navy Volunteer Reserve on 20 April 1917. He joined the Drake Battalion, on 30 August 1917 serving as an Able Seaman. Composed primarily of surplus Royal Navy reserves who were not required at sea.

The Drake Battalion war diary states that on 30 October 1917, they *'Supplied a party of six officers and 250 other ranks as stretcher bearers on account of 190th Brigade operations. Casualties - 3 other ranks killed and 1 other rank missing.'*

*New Irish Farm Cemetery*

Sidney Aish was one of those killed. He was subsequently laid to rest at plot IX. D. 14. within the New Irish Farm Cemetery.

# BURT AUTHURS

**Service Number:** 209212
**Rank:** Able Seaman
HMS Princess Irene
**Born:** 1875
**Died:** 27 May 1915
**Commemorated:**
Plymouth Naval Memorial

Albert William Authers was born in 1875 in the Devon village of Burlescombe, just a few miles from the Somerset border. Known as Burt, he married Harriot Ellis in Wellington in 1906 but by 1911 they were living in Bridgwater with their two children, Ellis and Alan. In 1913, Burt was registered as a Postman for North Petherton.

During the Great War, Burt served as an Able Seaman with the Royal Navy aboard the auxiliary minelayer *HMS Princess Irene*.

Built in Dumbarton by William Denny and Brothers Ltd, the 120m long *Princess Irene* was launched on 20 October 1914 as an Ocean Liner for the Princess fleet of the Canadian Pacific Railway Coast Service. Intending to serve on the Vancouver – Victoria – Seattle route, she was requisitioned by the Royal Navy on her completion in 1915 and converted into an auxiliary minelayer, with a complement of 225 officers and men.

On 27 May 1915, she was being loaded with mines in preparation for a mission whilst moored in Saltpan Reach, on the Medway Estuary in Kent, when disaster struck.

At 11:14, she exploded and disintegrated, sending a 100m column of flame and smoke shooting into the sky. Two munition barges moored alongside her were also destroyed.

*HMS Princess Irene*

The loss of life was horrendous, with a total of 352 people being killed, including 273 officers and men, and 76 dockyard workers who were on board the Princess Irene and the barges.

Hardly anything was left, with wreckage being sent up to 20 miles away and three civilians, including a nine year-old girl in the village of *Isle of Grain*, were sadly killed by flying debris.

Only one man onboard *HMS Princess Irene* survived, with very few bodies recovered. Albert 'Burt' Authers is commemorated on Panel 5 on the Plymouth Naval Memorial in Devon.

ABLE SEAMAN
AHERN A.
ANDREW E. J.
AUTHERS A. W.
BAILEY C.
BALDWIN W. E.
BANKIER G. H.

*Plymouth Naval Memorial*

# F. C. BANES-WALKER

**Service Number:**
**Rank:** Second Lieutenant
2nd Bn.,Devonshire Regiment
**Born:** 19 June 1888
**Died:** 9 May 1915
**Buried:** Le Trou Aid Post Cemetery
Fleurbaix, France

Frederick Cecil Banes-Walker was born on 19 June 1888 to Harry and Mary Alexandra Banes-Walker of 'Verriers', 43 Fore Street, North Petherton.

At the time, this was a very large single dwelling, indicating that the family had a certain amount of wealth. The 1891 census lists Harry as a *Gentleman Director* of a Brewery located in North Petherton on the site now occupied by Quantock Parade, which was literally across the road from the family home 'Verriers'. This house has since been divided up into smaller dwellings and is known as St Mary's Court.

At the age of twelve, Frederick was at Mr Coplestone's boarding school in Exmouth, and by the age of twenty-two he was gaining valuable business experience working at Ashton Gate Brewery in Bristol.

It would seem Frederick was a very competent sportsman. His younger years saw him play for Bridgwater Cricket Club, and as a capable hockey player, he was a member of the Gloucester County hockey team.

*Le Trou Aid Post Cemetery*

Before the outbreak of the Great War, Frederick was selected to represent Somerset County Cricket Club. He played 5 matches as a right handed batsman in 1914, scoring a total of 172 runs, with an average of 19.11 and a high score of 40.

In August 1914 he enlisted in the Gloucestershire Regiment but was offered a commission in the Devonshire Regiment a few weeks later. Frederick completed a machine-gun course and went out to France on 15 March 1915 as a machine-gun officer.

Frederick was killed in action just a few months later in the early morning of Sunday 9 May 1915 as the regiment were advancing under heavy cross-fire during the Battle of Aubers Ridge.

F. C. Banes-Walker was laid to rest in section F1 at Le Trou Aid Post Cemetery, on the outskirts of the small village of Fleurbaix, a few miles from where he fell.

*The final resting place of Frederick Banes-Walker*

# GERALD BANES-WALKER

**Service Number:**
**Rank:** Captain
      1st/5th Battalion,
      Somerset Light Infantry
**Born:** 15 November 1889
**Died:** 22 November 1917
**Buried:** Jerusalem War Cemetery

Gerald Banes-Walker was born on 15 November 1889 to Harry and Mary Alexandra Banes-Walker of 'Verriers', 43 Fore Street, North Petherton.

At the time, this was a very large single dwelling, indicating that the family had a certain amount of wealth. The 1891 census lists Harry as a *Gentleman Director* of a Brewery located in North Petherton on the site now occupied by Quantock Parade, which was literally across the road from the family home 'Verriers'. This house has since been divided up into smaller dwellings and is known as St Mary's Court.

At the age of eleven, Gerald was at Mr Coplestone's boarding school in Exmouth, and later boarded at Bradfield College, Berkshire, where he was a prefect and captain of the cricket eleven. By the age of twenty-one he was a boarder in the 23 room Burnham House, Hendon in London as he had secured a job working as a bank clerk at the Hong Kong and Shangai Bank.

At the outbreak of the Great War in 1914, Gerald enlisted with the Somerset Light Infantry and by 1915, he had risen to the rank of Lieutenant and was serving overseas in India.

The Officers of the 1/5th Bn. Somerset Light Infantry at Ambala (India) January 1915. Lt-Col Cooke-Hurle is in the centre of the middle row, with Major Brutton and Captain Calway on his right. On his left are Major Kite, and Captains Urwick, Major, Timms and Watson. In the back row Lieut Goodland is third from the right and Lieut Banes Walker stands behind the colonel. 2/Lieut Milsom sits on the right of the front row.

Gerald continued to serve with distinction and by 1917, had risen to the rank of Captain. Later that summer, he was transferred to Egypt and participated in the Palestine Campaign as part of the Egyptian Expeditionary Force. Fierce fighting saw them eventually gain a line about five kilometres west of Jerusalem on the 21 November 1917 and the following day, 22 November 1917, Gerald was killed in action.

*Jerusalem War Cemetery*

Gerald Banes-Walker was buried in plot X. 3. of the Jerusalem War Cemetery, which is located just to the north of the Old City of Jerusalem.

At the end of the Great War, the parents of Frederick and Gerald Banes-Walker paid for a stunning stained glass window to be installed in the chancel at St Mary's Church, North Petherton.

This must have cost a significant amount of money and is a poignant and lasting memorial to the two brothers.

# FREDERICK BINDING

**Service Number:** 26475
**Rank:** Rifleman
        18th Bn., Machine Gun Corps
**Born:** 1897
**Died:** 22 Nov 1918
**Buried:** Etretat Churchyard
        Extension, France

Frederick J Binding was born in 1897 to Albert and Emily Binding, who were living at Butts, North Petherton.

Frederick signed up on 23 August 1915 enrolling in the Machine Gun Corps as a rifleman. After eighteen months, he returned home from 6-15 January 1917 and he is recorded as suffering from trench foot from 21 January to 30 March 1917 - not uncommon for soldiers of the Great War. On 20 April 1918, Frederick joined the newly formed 18th Battalion Machine Gun Corps - formed from the Machine Gun Companies of 18th (Eastern) Division. At the time of the Armistice, the Division was in XIII Corps Reserve near La Cateau and Frederick was hospitalised.

Frederick died at 1st General Hospital, Entretat, on 22 November 1918 and is buried at plot III. F. 4. in the Etretat Churchyard Extension.

*Etretat Churchyard Extension*

# FREDERICK BOARD

**Service Number:** 9442
**Rank:** Private
      1st Battalion,
      Gloucestershire Regiment
**Born:** 1889
**Died:** 26 January 1917
**Buried:** Etaples Cemetery, France

Frederick Board was born in 1889 to Henry and Annie Board of Tappers Lane, North Petherton.

In 1911, at the age 19, Frederick had moved away and had enlisted with 1st Battalion, Gloucestershire Regiment, living at Cambridge Barracks, Portsmouth. At the outbreak of the Great War, the 1st Battalion were assigned to the 3rd Infantry Brigade, 1st Infantry Division, British Expeditionary Force, deploying on the Western Front and staying there for the duration of the conflict. They saw action at a number of the big battles, including the First and Second Battle of Ypres, the Battle of Aubers Ridge, the Battle of Loos, the Battle of Pozières and the Battle of the Somme.

Frederick died on 26 January 1917 and is buried at plot XXI. C. 11A. in Etaples Cemetery, along with over 11,000 other servicemen.

*Etaples Cemetery*

# HENRY CADDY

**Service Number:** 26846
**Rank:** Private
     4th Battalion,
     South Wales Borderers
**Born:** 1886
**Died:** 20 June 1916
**Commemorated:**
Basra Memorial, Iraq

Henry Caddy was born in 1886 at Haddon Farm Cottages, North Petherton and was baptised at St Mary's Church on 7 March 1886. At the age of 25, he was a wicker chair maker.

Initially, Henry enlisted in Bridgwater and joined the Somerset Light Infantry with the service number 20312. He then joined the 4th Battalion South Wales Borderers regiment, was given a the new service number of 26846 and served in the Asiatic theatre. They landed in Gallipoli on 15 July 1915 and engaged in various actions against the Turkish army including the Battle of Sari Bair. On 30 January 1916 the Battalion was deployed to Egypt to defend sections of the Suez Canal, before embarking for Mesopotamia (modern day Iraq) on 15 Feb 1916.

Henry Caddy died on 20 June 1916 and is remembered at the Basra Memorial, Iraq.

*Basra Memorial*

# GEORGE CHAMBERLAIN

**Service Number:** 10116
**Rank:** Private
8th Battalion
Devonshire Regiment
**Born:** 1886
**Died:** 25 September 1915
**Commemorated:** Loos Memorial,
Dud Corner Cemetery

George Chamberlain was born in early 1886 to William and Eliza Chamberlain who lived in Clavelshay, a short distance from North Petherton. He was baptised at St Mary's Church on 4 April 1886 and at the age of 15 he was a general labourer.

The outbreak of war offered George an opportunity to leave the life he knew as a labourer, and he joined up on 25 July 1915. Becoming a Private in the 8th Battalion, Devonshire Regiment, they left for France the very next day, landing in Le Havre.

George was killed on 25 September 1915 - the first day of the Battle of Loos, which was the biggest British attack of 1915. He is remembered on Panel 35 to 37 at the Loos Memorial at Dud Corner Cemetery, Nord-Pas-de-Calais.

*Loos Memorial, Dud Corner Cemetery*

# WALTER CHILCOTT

**Service Number:** 20565
**Rank:** Private
  6th Battalion,
  Dorsetshire Regiment
**Born:** 1900
**Died:** 08 June 1918
**Commemorated:** Pozieres
    Memorial, France

Walter Henry Chilcott was born to William and Sarah Chilcott of Tuckerton in North Newton in 1900. By 1911, Sarah and her children were living in a 3 room house in High Street, North Petherton.

Walter signed up with the 6th Battalion, Dorsetshire Regiment and soon found himself in France. The 6th Battalion had deployed to Boulogne in France in July 1915 as part of 50th Brigade in the 17th (Northern) Division and stayed on the Western Front for the duration of the war.

Walter Chilcott was recorded as presumed dead on 8 June 1918. His body was never found and he is remembered on Panel 48 at the Pozieres Memorial. He was 18 years old.

*Pozieres Memorial*

# ROBERT COCKRAM

**Service Number:** 4702
**Rank:** Private
        2nd/4th Battalion,
        Somerset Light Infantry
**Born:** 1890
**Died:** 10 August 1916.
**Buried:** Barrackpore New Cemetery
        India

Robert James Cockram was born to William and Mary Cockram in South Moulton, Devon before the family moved to a five room house in Farringdon, North Petherton.

Robert enlisted with the Somerset Light Infantry at Wells and joined the 2nd/4th Battalion. They were originally formed in September 1914 as a duplicate of the 4th Battalion, and became part of the much bigger 45th (2nd Wessex) Division.

The 2nd/4th Battalion of the Somerset Light Infantry, were a Territorial Force - essentially troops that were deemed unfit for front line duty, and they were sent to India so that the regular units there could be released for service in France.

The Government of India agreed to send 32 British and 20 Indian regular army battalions to Europe in exchange for 43 Territorial Force battalions in order to maintain the status quo.

With this in mind, the 45th Division sailed from Southampton on 25 November 1914 heading for India. Some went to Karachi (Pakistan) via Aden, landing on 9 January 1915, with the rest landing at Bombay (modern day Mumbai) later that month.

Robert was one of these. He travelled across India to Kolkata and then onto the administrative and military centre of Barrackpore, which is around twenty miles to the north of Kolkata.

For the next eighteen months Robert was stationed at the military camp in Barrackpore, undertaking various guard duties.

Robert died of Cholera whilst at Barrackpore in India on 10 August 1916 and is buried at Plot 4. Row 7. Grave 1344. in Barrackpore New Cemetery.

*Barrackpore New Cemetery*

The following poem was printed in the Bridgwater Mercury on 29th August 1916 by his parents:

*Sleep on, dear one, in a foreign grave,*
*Your life for your country you nobly gave;*
*The parting was sad, the blow severe;*
*To part with one we loved so dear.*
*We little thought when leaving home*
*That he would ne'er return;*
*But now he lies in a soldier's grave,*
*And we are left to mourn.*

# SYDNEY CROCKER

**Service Number:** T/094206
**Rank:** Driver
1st Coy. 41st Div.
Train, Army Service Corps
**Born:** 1895
**Died:** 17 April 1918
**Buried:** Gwalia Cemetery, Belgium

Sydney Crocker was born to John and Mary Crocker, and lived in Chicks Cottage, Fitzhead. By the time he was sixteen, Sydney was working as a farm labourer and the family were living in a four room house at Standards, North Petherton.

Sydney joined the army at Aldershot on 3 May 1915. He served with 1st Company, 41st Division Train, Army Service Corps as a driver and was deployed in both France and Italy.

Sydney was wounded whilst on duty on 5 January 1918, but recovered from his injuries and returned to the front line. He was killed in action in the field in on 17 April 1918.

Sydney is buried at plot II. H. 7. in Gwalia Cemetery, Belgium, a few miles from the town of Ypres.

*Gwalia Cemetery*

# CHARLES DYMOND

**Service Number:** 17756
**Rank:** Private
    1st Battalion
    Somerset Light Infantry
**Born:** 1876
**Died:** 01 July 1916.
**Commemorated:**
Thiepval Memorial, France

Charles Dymond was born in 1876 in Lyng, Somerset to Charles and Ann Dymond. At 16, he was an agricultural labourer. Charles married Helen, who was from North Petherton, in 1905 and by 1911 they were living at 1 Bathurst Road, Milton, Weston in a 5 room house.

Charles joined the 1st Battalion, Somerset Light Infantry and was deployed to France. On 1 July 1916 at 7.30 am, fourteen British Divisions, including the 1st battalion, attacked the enemy on the first day of the Battle of the Somme. 26 officers and 478 men of the 1st battalion, Somerset Light Infantry were killed, missing or wounded - Charles was missing in action, assumed dead. He was never found.

*Thiepval Memorial*

Charles Dymond is remembered on Pier and Face 2 A of the Thiepval Memorial, which has the names of over 72,000 men with no known grave.

# EDWIN ELVER

**Service Number:** 6694
**Rank:** Private
       1st Battalion,
       Somerset Light Infantry
**Born:** 1886
**Died:** 26 August 1914
**Commemorated:** La Ferte-sous-Jouarre memorial, Ile de France

Edwin John Elver was born in 1886 in Walton, Somerset to Thomas and Eliza Elver. At 15, Edwin was a shoemaker working from the family home, which was then at Ashcott. He married Annie West, of North Petherton on 5 August 1907 and they moved into a four room house in the High Street, North Petherton.

Edwin signed up with the 1st Battalion of the Somerset Light Infantry at the very beginning of the war and was sent to France as part of the British Expeditionary Forces on 21st August 1914. He was killed on 26 August 1914 during the battle of Le Cateau, just 4 days after arriving in France, and only 20 days after the beginning of the war.

Edwin John Elver is remembered on the La Ferté-sous-Jouarre Memorial, which is located around 40 miles to the east of Paris.

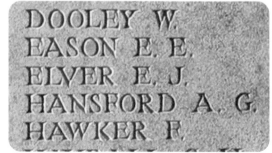

*La Ferte-sous-Jouarre memorial*

# R J C FERGUSON

**Service Number:** 21528
**Rank:** Corporal
     1st Battalion
     Oxford & Bucks Light Infantry
**Born:** 01 April 1879
**Died:** 09 January 1919
**Commemorated:**
Kirkee 1914-1918 Memorial, India

Robert, known as James to his friends and family, was born to Robert Alexander and Lynda Rydon Ferguson on 01 April 1879 in North Petherton. A few years later they moved Chilton Street, Wembdon, but by 1891, James was recorded as living with his uncle, James Nation, of Millcombe Mills, in North Petherton as his parents had moved to America.

In 1901, James was an assistant teacher in Twickenham and by 1911 he was a  school teacher in Stogursey, before signing up at the outbreak of war in 1914.

He served with the 1st Battalion, Oxford & Bucks Light Infantry in Bombay, India, where he died of disease in January 1919.

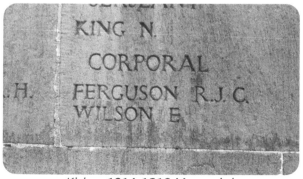

James Ferguson is commemorated on Face D of the Kirkee 1914-1918 Memorial in the town of Poona on the Plateau above Bombay.

*Kirkee 1914-1918 Memorial*

# CHARLES FERMOR

**Service Number:** 22387
**Rank:** Private
　　　　14th Battalion,
　　　　Royal Warwickshire Regiment
**Born:** 01 August 1889
**Died:** 04 October 1917
**Buried:** Tyne Cot Cemetery, Belgium

Charles Fermor was born at Withyham in Sussex on 01 August 1889 to Arthur Fermor and Charlotte Pilbeam. In 1908 they moved to Broomfield, near North Petherton, where his father worked as a second gamekeeper.

At the age of 21, Charles was living at Hurley in Berkshire working as a gamekeeper, and a few years later in 1913, he married Alice Gardner, who came from North Petherton. They had three children, Cecil, born in October 1914; Alice, born in December 1915; and Ida born in January 1917.

Charles served with 14th Battalion Royal Warwickshire Regiment and was killed during the Third Battle of Ypres, where more than 250,000 allied soldiers were lost between July and November 1917.

Charles is buried in plot LVIII. E. 12. of the Tyne Cot Cemetery, Belgium, along with nearly 12,000 others.

*Tyne Cot Cemetery, Belgium*

# ALBERT GADD

**Service Number:** 26733
**Rank:** Private
     6th Battalion
     Somerset Light Infantry
**Born:** 04 August 1897
**Died:** 26 August 1917
**Commemorated:**
Tyne Cot Memorial, Belgium

Albert George Gadd was born to Samuel and Eliza Gadd of The Steam Bakery, North Petherton. Baptised at St Mary's Church in the town on 24 September 1897, they lived in Fore Street and Albert attended North Petherton school until April 1909 when he went to Dr Morgan's Grammar School in Bridgwater.

When war broke out, Albert went to Taunton and enlisted with the 6th Battalion Somerset Light Infantry. In 1917, they were involved in the German retreat to the Hindenburg Line, the Arras Offensive and the Third Battle of Ypres. It was during this battle that Albert was wounded on 23 August 1917 and sadly died a few days later on 26 August 1917. He was 20 years old.

FROST C. E.
FRY R.
GADD A. G.
GAMMON J.
GARNER H.

*Tyne Cot Memorial*

Albert Gadd is commemorated on panel 41-42 of the Tyne Cot Memorial in Belgium, along with 35,000 others whose final resting places are not known.

# WILLIAM GARDNER

**Service Number:** 5896
**Rank:** Sergeant
1st/5th Battalion,
Somerset Light Infantry
**Born:** 1882
**Died:** 06 October 1917
**Buried:** Gaza War Cemetery

William John Gardner was born in 1882 to Matthew and Mary Gardner of Tappers Lane, North Petherton. As a child he attended North Petherton school and during this time the family moved to Fore Street.

William joined the Somerset Light Infantry in 1898 when he was just 16 years old, and lived at Jellalabad Barracks in Taunton. By the time war broke out in 1914, William had been in the army for sixteen years and became a drill sergeant at Taunton Barracks.

*View of Jellalabad Barracks (now flats) from Vivary Park, Taunton*

A newspaper article of the time indicates that he went on to train officers at Sandhurst Military Academy, and could have remained in England for the duration of the war, but that his *great ambition was to go to The Front.*

In May 1917, his battalion was sent to Egypt and participated in the Palestine Campaign as part of the Egyptian Expeditionary Force. William Gardener was killed while gallantly attacking the Turkish line on 06 October 1917 and it was reported that *'Major D. S. Watson and Lieut. Victor Helps, local officers of the Somersets to which Sergeant Gardener was attached, speak very highly of the deceased's value as a non-commissioned officer, and of his reckless daring.'*

*Gaza War Cemetery*

At the time of his death, William was recorded as the husband of Mrs Gardener of Verno Lodge, 23 Hamilton Road, Boscombe, Bournemouth. He is buried at plot XVI. G. 15. at the Gaza War Cemetery, along with over 3,000 other Commonwealth soldiers.

# FREDERICK GRAY

**Service Number:** 21323
**Rank:** Lance Corporal
        8th Battalion,
        Somerset Light Infantry
**Born:** 1892
**Died:** 11 April 1917
**Commemorated:** Arras Memorial,
                France

Frederick Louis Gray was born in 1892 to James and Elizabeth Gray living at Butts, North Petherton. By 1911 the family had moved to North Street and nineteen year old Frederick was a wicker chair maker.

In 1914, Frederick was employed as a postman between Bridgwater and North Petherton, but then decided to enlist in the army in February 1916, initially as Private 36031 in the Wiltshire Regiment.

*The Arras Memorial*

For some reason he then became Private 21323 with the 8th Battalion Somerset Light Infantry, and after initial training, was sent to the Western Front in May 1916.

*Arras Memorial*

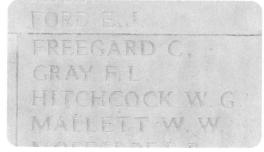

Frederick was killed during an advance on Easter Monday, with his death being officially recorded as 11 April 1917.

A letter to his parents, which was subsequently reported in the local Bridgwater Mercury, states that *'Lance-Corporal Gray was killed in action on or about April 9th during some hard fighting. The deceased soldier and two or three others were taking cover in a shell hole from the German guns when a shall exploded in their midst, killing them all.'*

Frederick Gray has no known grave and is commemorated on panel 4 of the Arras Memorial.

# EDMOND HILL

**Service Number:** 36393
**Rank:** Private
      3rd Battalion,
      Worcestershire Regiment
**Born:** 1877
**Died:** 27 May 1918
**Commemorated:** Soissons
                Memorial, France

Edmond Hill was born to Henry and Edith Hill sometime in 1877 and was baptised a few years later on 12 October 1879 at St Peter's Church, North Newton.

In 1901, his parents had moved to a hamlet of North Newton called Chadmead, and twenty-four year old Edmond still lived with them, working as a gardener. On 19th March 1912 Edmund married Alice Clatworthy and they lived in Newton Road, North Petherton.

*Soissons Memorial*

They had two children: daughter Edith being born on 18 May 1913 and Freda being born on 09 December 1914.

Edmund enlisted with the army on 27 November 1915 at Taunton. He joined the 3rd Battalion Worcester Regiment as Private 36393. He was wounded in April 1916 and returned home for five months between June and October 1916, presumably to convalesce. Records show that he spent another period at home from February to June 1917, before retuning to the Western Front.

Edmond was listed as missing on 11 April 1918.

*Heavy artillery near Soissons, 1918*

After more than six weeks missing, he was presumed dead on 27 May 1918.

Edmond Hill is commemorated on the Soissons War Memorial, along with nearly 4,000 others who were killed in the area between May and August 1918, and have no known grave.

*Soissons Memorial*

# HAROLD HOUSE

**Service Number:** J/30184
**Rank:** Ordinary Seaman
            HMS Queen Mary
**Born:** 11 November 1897
**Died:** 31 May 1916
**Commemorated:** Plymouth Naval
            Memorial

Harold House was born on 11 November 1897 to Ellen House - a single woman - and was baptised a month later on 11 December, at St Mary's Church in North Petherton. Harold initially lived with his grandmother Elizabeth and his Uncle Charles. Ellen later married a widower, George West, and by 1911, thirteen year old Harold was back living with his Mother and Step-Father at Compass Cottage in North Petherton.

He joined the Royal Navy on 18 March 1914 at the age of 16, serving on the training ship *Impregnable* as Boy, 2nd class.

*HMS Queen Mary*

Harold was promoted to Boy, 1st Class in October 1914 and joined the battlecruiser *HMS Queen Mary* on 30 October 1914. On 11 November 1915 he was promoted to *Ordinary Seaman*.

*Plymouth Naval Memorial*

On 31 May 1916, *HMS Queen Mary* and the rest of the 1st Battlecruiser Fleet were sent to intercept a sortie by the German High Seas Fleet into the North Sea, not far from Jutland.

She was hit by the German battlecruiser *Derfflinger* during the early part of the battle and her magazines exploded - sinking the ship. There were only 20 survivors from the 1,289 crew.

Harold House was just 19 when he was killed. His body was never recovered and he is commemorated on panel 13 of the Plymouth Naval Memorial.

# ERNEST MARKS

**Service Number:** 240245
**Rank:** Private
      1st/5th Battalion
      Somerset Light Infantry
**Born:** 25 January 1895
**Died:** 12 October 1917
**Buried:** Kantara War Memorial
      Cemetery, Egypt

Ernest Marks was born on 25 January 1895 in Back Lane, North Petherton to Emily Marks - there was no named father. They resided with his uncle (Emily's brother) John Marks.

At the age of sixteen, Ernest was a mason's labourer, before signing up with the Somerset Light Infantry at the outbreak of the war in 1914.

In May 1917, his battalion was sent to Egypt and participated in the Palestine Campaign as part of the Egyptian Expeditionary Force. Ernest died of disease on 12 October 1917 whilst in Egypt and was buried in plot E. 90. at the Kantara War Memorial Cemetery in the Sinai Peninsula, on the east bank of the Suez Canal.

The Kantara War Memorial Cemetery contains 1,562 Commonwealth burials from the First World War and 110 from the Second World War.

*Kantara War Memorial Cemetery*

# PATRICK MARKS

**Service Number:** 11659
**Rank:** Private
      1st Battalion
      Grenadier Guards
**Born:** 1883
**Died:** 26 October 1914
**Commemorated:**
Menin Gate, Ypres, Belgium

Patrick Marks was born to Richard and Mary Marks in 1883 and lived at 47 Farringdon, North Petherton. In 1901, eighteen year old Patrick was a mason's labourer and lived with his brother, John Marks, in Back Lane. He was an uncle to Ernest Marks.

In 1904, twenty-one year old Patrick enlisted in Cardiff and was initially in the 3rd Battalion Grenadier Guards. Listed as an orderly room clerk, by 1911 he was living at Wellington Barracks, St James' Park, Westminster. Patrick was amongst the first of the British troops to fight in the Great War and was killed in action in Flanders on 26 October 1914. His body was never found and he is commemorated on Panel 9 and 11 of the Menin Gate, Ypres, Belgium.

LOGAN P.
McGANN F.
McGILLIVRAY A.
MARKS P.
MASTERS E. G.
MATCHAM E.
MATHER J.

*Menin Gate, Ypres*

Nearly 55,000 men are listed on the Menin Gate. Each night at 8 pm, the traffic is stopped and buglers sound the Last Post in the roadway under the Memorial's arches.

# ALFRED MILLER

**Service Number:** 14776
**Rank:** Corporal
      8th Battalion
      Somerset Light Infantry
**Born:** 1891
**Died:** 14 November 1916
**Commemorated:** Thiepval Memorial,
France

Alfred Miller was born in 1891 to James and Elizabeth Miller in Angel Row in the village of Fivehead. In 1911, at the age of twenty, Alfred was working as a waggoner and still lived with his parents and siblings, now at Great Thorne Cottage, Huntstile, Goathurst.

Alfred served in the 8th Battalion of the Somerset Light Infantry and gained promotion to the rank of Corporal. In 1916, he saw action in *The Battle of the Somme*, and on the 08 July 1916 the battalion transferred with 63rd Brigade to 37th Division. Alfred was killed on 14 November 1916. His body was never found and he is commemorated on Pier and Face 2 A of the Thiepval Memorial in France.

Alfred's parents were living in Clare Street, North Petherton at the time of his death, but it seems that Alfred is also remembered on the Fivehead War Memorial.

*Thiepval Memorial, France*

# WALTER NORLEY

**Service Number:** 82418
**Rank:** Gunner
      84th Siege Battery
      Royal Garrison Artillery
**Born:** 1897
**Died:** 17 April 1917
**Buried:** Salonika (Lembert Road)
      Military Cemetery, Greece

Walter Robert Norley was born in 1897 at 117 Huntworth to George and Maria Norley and at the age of fourteen was a general farm labourer.

Walter enlisted with the Army Reserves on 06 December 1915 at the age of eighteen. On 25 May 1916 he was called for active service and was a Gunner with the 84th Siege Battery, Royal Garrison Artillery. They were equipped with heavy howitzers, sending large calibre high explosive shells onto the enemy. On 08 January 1917, they relocated to Salonika (now Thessalonika), Greece and the town was the base of the British Salonika Force. Walter died of wounds received on 17 April 1917, aged 20.

*Salonika (Lembert Road) Military Cemetery*

Walter was buried in plot 959 in the Salonika (Lembert Road) Military Cemetery at Thessalonika along with over 1,600 other soldiers.

# WILLIAM NORTHCOMBE

**Service Number:** R/1184
**Rank:** Able Seaman
      Drake Battalion
      RN Volunteer Reserve
**Born:** 08 November 1886
**Died:** 07 October 1918
**Buried:** Terlincthun British
Cemetery, Wimille, France

William Northcombe was born on 08 November 1886 to Edwin and Ellen Northcombe. They lived at Hyde Park Corner in North Petherton and he attended the town's school. During the first few years of his life, the family moved to the Old Turnpike Road, before returning to Hyde Park Corner by 1911.

William worked as a painter and banns were read for William and Dorcas Beck from Stoke St Gregory in April 1912. They wed soon after, and their first son, Henry, was born on 17 October 1914. On 05 June 1916, William became an army reservist and the couple welcomed their second child, Percy, on 5 March 1917.

William was drafted for the British Expeditionary Forces on 06 August 1917, and joined the Drake Battalion, Royal Navy.

*14th General Hospital, Wimereux, France*

William went across the English Channel to the Western Front and in October 1917, he suffered multiple gunshot wounds and was later invalided back to England on 07 November 1917. It would seem that William made a good recovery as he was then re-drafted for the British Expeditionary Force, again with the Drake Battalion on 11 March 1918.

*Terlincthun British Cemetery*

On 28 September 1918, William received wounds to the abdomen and was taken from the front line to the 14th General Hospital at Wimereux. It was here that he sadly succumbed to his injuries and died on 07 October 1918.

William Northcombe was buried in plot IV. F. 20. at the Terlincthun British Cemetery, Wimille, France - just to the south of Wimereux. The cemetery contains over 4,000 Commonwealth burials from the First World War.

The bells of St Mary's Church tolled upon hearing the sad news - as they did every time a man from the town was lost.

# ALFRED PIKE

**Service Number:** G/3383
**Rank:** Sergeant
9th Battalion
Royal Sussex Regiment
**Born:** 1891
**Died:** 10 May 1916
**Buried:** Bailleul Communal
Cemetery Extension, Nord, France

Alfred Pike was born in 1891 to William and Maria Pike who lived in Thurloxton. By the 1901 census the family were now living at Huntworth Gate in North Petherton, with Alfred attending the local school, before becoming a farm labourer like his father.

Alfred enlisted at the outbreak of the war in Littlehampton, Sussex and joined the 9th Battalion of the Royal Sussex Regiment - who were formed at Chichester.

*Bailleul Communal Cemetery Extension, Nord*

All original recruits were given a 'G' prefix to their regimental number; as in Alfred's case. After their formation, the battalion went into camp on the South Downs around Brighton where they seemingly took part in recruitment marches on the seafront! In December 1914 the battalion moved to Portslade, followed by Shoreham in April 1915 and then to Woking, Surrey in June 1915.

*Bailleul Communal Cemetery Ext*

The 9th Battalion landed in France, at Boulogne, on 31 August 1915. They fought in The Battle of Loos that September, suffering heavy casualties.

Alfred was wounded in a German Gas attack at Wulverghem on 30 April 1916, and sadly died on 10 May 1916.

He is buried at plot II. B. 82. at the Bailleul Communal Cemetery Extension, Nord, along with over 4,000 other soldiers of the Great War. Bailleul is a large town near the Belgian border and was an important railway and air depot as well as a hospital centre.

# ROBERT PIKE

**Service Number:** 186904
**Rank:** Lance Bombardier
Royal Garrison Artillery
'Q' Anti Aircraft Battery
**Born:** 1888
**Died:** 03 September 1918
**Buried:** Dernancourt Communal
Cemetery Extension, France

Robert Henry Pike was born in 1888 to William and Maria Pike who lived in Thurloxton. He was the older brother of Alfred Pike. By the 1901 census the family were now living at Huntworth Gate in North Petherton, with Robert being listed as a farm boy.

In the summer of 1913, Robert married Rose Butler in Chesterfield and moved north to start their new life in Derbyshire.

*An anti-aircraft unit, 1918*

Once the war had started, Robert signed up and joined the Royal Garrison Artillery. He joined 'Q' anti aircraft battery who were part of Third Army in France. In April 1918 they served with 1st Anzac Corps in the Somme and Robert became a Lance Bombardier.

Robert was wounded and sadly died on 03 September 1918. He was buried at plot VIII. B. 3. in the Dernancourt Communal Cemetery Extension in France. The village of Dernancourt is around two miles from the larger town of Albert. Designed by Sir Edwin Lutyens, the extension contains over two thousand Commonwealth burials and commemorations of the First World War.

Robert's wife, Rose, remained living in Tamworth Street, Duffield, Derby and Robert's parents, who were still living in North Petherton, had his name included on the war memorial of the town of his birth.

*Dernancourt Communal Cemetery Extension, France*

# WILFRED RIDGE

**Service Number:** 65351
**Rank:** Shoeing Smith
Royal Field Artillery
D Battery, 94th Brigade
**Born:** 16 March 1896
**Died:** 27 May 1918
**Buried:** Hermonville Military
Cemetery, France

Wilfred James Ridge was born on 16 March 1896 to James and Alice Ridge who lived in Fore Street, North Petherton. He attended North Petherton council elementary school, before becoming a day boarder at Dr Morgan's Grammar School in Bridgwater, and later joining the family blacksmith business in North Petherton.

On 03 December 1914, Wilfred signed up as a shoeing smith in 'D' Battery, 94th Brigade in the Royal Field Army. He was killed in action on 27 May 1918 and is buried at plot III. D. 9. at Hermonville Military Cemetery in France.

*Hermonville Military Cemetery, France*

# GEORGE ROBERTS

**Service Number:** 42433
**Rank:** Private
      7th Battalion
      Lincolnshire Regiment
**Born:** 1891
**Died:** 18 September 1918
**Commemorated:** Vis-en-Artois
            Memorial, France

George Henry Roberts was born in 1891 to John and Eliza Roberts in Salford, Greater Manchester. His parents were originally from Bridgwater and North Newton and by 1901 they moved to Bull Street in Creech St Michael.

At the age of 20, George was a boarder back up in Lancashire where he was working as a coal miner, and his parents had moved to Churchill Cottage in North Newton.

George signed up to the 7th Battalion, Lincolnshire Regiment and was killed in the advance in Picardy and Artois on 18 September 1918. He is remembered on Panel 4 of the Vis-en-Artois Memorial. This Memorial bears the names of nearly 10,000 men who fell from August 1918 to November 1918, and who have no known grave. George's brothers, Thomas and William, were also killed during the Great War.

*Vis-en-Artois Memorial, France*

# THOMAS ROBERTS

**Service Number:** 9501
**Rank:** Private
    1st Battalion
    Somerset Light Infantry
**Born:** 1896
**Died:** 26 August 1914
**Buried:** Fontaine-Au-Pire Communal
    Cemetery, France

Thomas Roberts was born in 1896 to John and Eliza Roberts in St Helens, Merseyside. His parents were originally from Bridgwater and North Newton and by 1901 they had moved to Bull Street in Creech St Michael.

At the age of 15, Thomas was working as a labourer, and the family had moved to Churchill cottage in North Newton.

Thomas enlisted with the 1st Battalion of the Somerset Light Infantry on 21 August 1914 and around the same time, his parents had moved again, this time to New Inn Plott, North Petherton. The Battalion arrived in France as part of the British Expeditionary Forces on 22 August 1914 - just a day after Thomas had enlisted. British and French troops had suffered defeats at the Battle of Charleroi (21–23 August) and

the Battle of Mons (23 August) so the 1st Battalion, as part of the British II Corps, fought a delaying action at Le Cateau to slow down the German pursuit.

*Le Cateau, 1914*

The battle began at dawn on 26 August 1914, with a German artillery barrage across nearly eight miles of essentially open ground held by the British, lasting until noon. At this point, the German infantry began to advance, and fierce fighting erupted which lasted until late afternoon, when the British were able to organise a strategic withdrawal. Although they had managed to slow the German infantry's advance, losses were incredibly high on both sides - with over 7,800 British casualties from this one day's fighting.

Thomas was one of those to lose his life - he was just 20 years old. Initially, like many others, he was posted as missing in action after the engagement, but in the days and weeks that followed his body was identified. His death came just twenty days after the beginning of the war and just four days after he had arrived in France with his battalion. He is buried at plot I. A. 67. at the Fontaine-Au-Pire Communal Cemetery

Fontaine-Au-Pire is a large village seven miles from the town of Cambrai. The cemetery has 70 Commonwealth burials there.

*Fontaine-Au-Pire Communal Cemetery*

# WILLIAM ROBERTS

**Service Number:** 3/6762
**Rank:** Private
    1st Battalion
    Machine Gun Section
    Somerset Light Infantry
**Born:** 1898
**Died:** 06 July 1915
**Buried:** Ferme-Olivier Cemetery,
    Belgium

William Roberts was born in 1898 to John and Eliza Roberts in St Helens, Merseyside. His parents were originally from Bridgwater and North Newton and by 1901 they had moved to Bull Street in Creech St Michael.

The family moved to Churchill cottage in North Newton and then to New Inn Plott, North Petherton around the time of the outbreak of the Great War.

In August 1914, the Roberts' family received the sad news that William's elder brother Thomas had been killed in the fighting near Cambrai. William himself then joined up in Exeter on 11 November 1914, to the same battalion that Thomas had been in - possibly motivated by the death of his brother.

He joined as a Private in the Machine Gun Section of the 1st Battalion, Somerset Light Infantry - where training would involve a wooden mock-up machine-gun.

*Somerset Light Infantry training*

With the battalion already abroad, as soon as William had completed his training, he went across to France and fought in the Second Battle of Ypres between 22 April – 25 May 1915 in an effort to control the high ground above the town.

On 06 July 1915, the 1st Battalion suffered a day-long barrage of shelling from the Germans, and it was during this onslaught that William Roberts was killed. He was 17 years old.

As reported in the Bridgwater Mercury on 21 July 1915, the Free Church chaplain attached to the 1st Battalion wrote to William's parents *"It is my sad task to inform you that your loved one passed away on the night of July 6th at our ambulance. When I was called to him he was beyond speaking to. There was no hope for him, as he was wounded in several places and had lost much blood. May God support you in this time of sorrow."*

William is buried at Plot 1. Row K. Grave 10. at the Ferme-Olivier Cemetery, Belgium, along with 400 other fallen soldiers.

*Ferme-Olivier Cemetery, Belgium*

# THOMAS RUCKLEY

**Service Number:** 235019
**Rank:** Private
15th Battlion
Hampshire Regiment
**Born:** 1898
**Died:** 09 August 1918
**Buried:** La Clytte Military Cemetery, Belgium

Thomas Albert Ruckley was born in 1898 to Elias and Mary Ruckley of Back Lane, North Petherton. They moved to North Street and Thomas attended North Petherton Council School.

Thomas initially signed up in Taunton with the Somerset Light Infantry before joining the 15th Battalion of the Hampshire Regiment. He was praised by the Major-General of the Hampshire's for *'gallantry and devotion to duty'* during fighting on 20 September 1917.

Thomas Ruckley was killed on 09 August 1918 and is buried at plot IV. D. 24. of the La Clytte Military Cemetery, Belgium.

*La Clytte Military Cemetery, Belgium*

# WILLIAM RUCKLEY

**Service Number:** 13742
**Rank:** Private
      10th Battalion
      Devonshire Regiment
**Born:** 1886
**Died:** 10 February 1917
**Commemorated:** Dorian Memorial
                Cemetery, Greece

William Ruckley was born in 1886 to to Elias and Mary Ruckley of Back Lane, North Petherton. He attended North Petherton Council School and became a wicker worker.

William joined the Army at the outbreak of war, and participated in several engagements on the Western Front. He was later transferred to the Balkans, where he was killed at Salonika, Greece, on 10 February 1917. His body was never found. His commanding officer wrote: *Ruckley was one of a bombing party, very few of whom returned. I have made careful enquiries from all with the company who are likely to know anything as to his fate. No one actually saw him fall, but his rifle was found and brought back. It is believed that he and Pte. Robinson were together and hit by the same bomb. Ruckley was a good soldier, and of a most cheerful disposition.* William is remembered on the Dorian Memorial.

*Dorian Memorial Cemetery, Greece*

# GEORGE SALTER

**Service Number:** 26611
**Rank:** Private
    8th Battlion
    Somerset Light Infantry
**Born:** 1885
**Died:** 23 April 1917
**Buried:** Canadian Cemetery, No. 2,
    Neuville-Saint-Vaast, France

George Salter was born in 1885 to Charles and Mary-Ann Salter of New Yard, Northmoor Green in the parish of North Petherton.

In 1909, George, a wicker chair maker, married Mary, a dress maker from Exford. They wed on Christmas Day at Otterhampton due to the fact they were both living at Combwich at the time. George signed up to the 8th Battalion of the Somerset Light Infantry, and was killed in action on 23rd April 1917. He is buried at plot 16. G. 2. at the Canadian Cemetery, No. 2, Neuville-Saint-Vaast, France.

*Canadian Cemetery, No. 2, Neuville-Saint-Vaast, France*

# WILLIAM SPENDER

**Service Number:** 97350
**Rank:** Sapper
      Cable Section
      Royal Engineers
**Born:** 1879
**Died:** 01 February 1919
**Commemorated:** Chatby Memorial,
                    Alexandria, Egypt

William John Clatworthy Spender was born in 1879 to James and Mary Spender, who were living in Kensington, London. The family moved to North Petherton and in 1901, 22 year-old William, who was now a carpenter, was living on the High Street with his father and his step-mother Jane. In 1904, he married dressmaker Elizabeth Hunt. They lived at Hyde park Corner and had three children: Geoffrey, Stanley and Arthur.

William was a Sapper with the Royal Engineers, Cable Section and drowned 01 February 1919 when the Trawler *John Roberts* sunk between Melina and Alexandria. He is commemorated on the Chatby Memorial, Alexandria in Egypt.

*Chatby Memorial, Alexandria, Egypt*

# WALTER SPILLER

**Service Number:** J/43626
**Rank:** Boy 1st Class
H.M.S. Vanguard
**Born:** 1900
**Died:** 09 July 1917
**Commemorated:** Chatham Naval
Memorial

Walter John Spiller was born in 1900 to John and Naomi Spiller of Hammet Street, North Petherton.

Walter signed up with the Royal Navy just as soon as he was allowed and progessed quickly to *Boy 1st Class*. This rank was for a boy aged 16 to 18, who had previously served for between 9 months and 18 months rated as *'boy 2nd class'* and had shown sufficient proficiency in seamanship and accumulated at least one good conduct badge.

*HMS Vanguard*

*Chatham Memorial*

Walter then served on HMS Vanguard, a St Vincent-class dreadnought battleship. On the night of 09 July 1917, HMS Vanguard was anchored in Scapa Flow in the Orkney Islands, Scotland, when an internal explosion destroyed the ship - killing all but two of the 845 men aboard. Walter was one of these - he was 17. Walter Spiller is remembered on the Chatham Naval Memorial.

# GEORGE THRESHER

**Service Number:** 32296
**Rank:** Private
      1st Battalion
      Northamptonshire Regiment
**Born:** 1894
**Died:** 18 October 1918
**Buried:** Vadencourt British
        Cemetery, France

George Thresher was born in 1894 to Frederick and Alice Thresher of High Street, North Petherton.

He signed up on 17 September 1915 but it wasn't until 26 March 1916 that he joined up with the British Expeditionary Force in France. He was injured and returned home between 13 September 1916 and 10 February 1917 - during this time he married Alice Burrows. He was sent home a further two times due to injuries: 28 March-19 August 1917 and 6 December 1917-10 February 1918. George died on 18 October 1918 at 47 Casualty Clearing Station of wounds received. He was buried at plot II. C. 15. Vadencourt British Cemetery, France. He never saw his daughter, Sylvia, who was born at the end of 1918

*Vadencourt British Cemetery, France*

# FRANK UPHAM

**Service Number:** 7490
**Rank:** Private
      1st Battalion
      Somerset Light Infantry
**Born:** 1887
**Died:** 24 May 1915
**Buried:** Duhallow A.D.S. Cemetery,
      Belgium

Frank Upham was born in 1887 to David and Susan Upham who were living in Spaxton. At the age of 14, Frank, still living at the family home, was working as a Telegraph boy.

By the 1911 census, 24 year-old Frank had moved, and was one of numerous residents at a house in Henry Place, Dock Ward, County Antrim, earning a living as a general labourer.

At some point before the outbreak of the war, Frank's parents returned to North Petherton - and so did Frank. He signed up at Taunton and served with the 1st Battalion of the Somerset Light Infantry, who arrived in France with the BEF on 22 August 1914, and remained on the Western Front until 1918.

*The city of Ypres after the Second Battle of Ypres*

During 1914, the battalion saw action in *The Battle of the Marne*, *The Battle of the Aisne* and *The Battle of Messines*. In 1915, they fought in *The Second Battle of Ypres (22 April-25 May 1915)*, with the the final engagement being the *Battle of Bellewaarde* (24–25 May).

On 24 May the Germans released a gas attack that hit Shell Trap Farm and it was during this attack that Frank was killed.

*Duhallow A.D.S. Cemetery*

He is buried at plot VI. A. 1. at Duhallow A.D.S. Cemetery.

**Herbert John Webley.**

# HERBERT WEBLEY

**Service Number:**
**Rank:** Lieutenant
HMS Paragon
**Born:** 06 September 1883
**Died:** 17 March 1917
**Commemorated:** Portsmouth Naval Memorial

Herbert John Webley was born on 06 September 1883 to Frank and Emma Webley at Grays in Essex. His father was the Chief Officer on a Training Ship and Herbert followed him into the navy at the age of 15 in 1898, joining H. M. Training Ship St. Vincent.

Herbert married Emma Burnett, who was orignially from Thurloxton, at St Mary's Church, Bridgwater on 28 September 1907 and the had their first child, Leila, in 1908.

Herbert was appointed Warrant Officer in July 1909 and whilst serving on HMS Excellent, formed one of the Gun Carriage Crew at the funeral of King Edward VII on Friday 20 May 1910.

By 1911 they were living at Baymead, North Petherton and welcomed their second child, Arthur, in 1912.

*Funeral of King Edward VII, 1910*

*HMS Paragon*

Herbert served on *HMS Royal Yacht*; *HMS Crescent*; *HMS Venus*; *HMS Revenge* and *HMS Natal*, before he was then appointed *Mate* on 01 May 1914.

Herbert was posted to *HMS Sylvia* at the outbreak of war in August 1914. On 01 May 1916 he was promoted to the rank of Lieutenant and at the same time, joined the 917 ton Acasta-class destroyer *HMS Paragon*.

*Portsmouth Naval Memorial*

On 17 March 1917, *HMS Paragon*, alongside the destroyer *HMS Llewellyn*, engaged eight German torpedo boats in the Dover Strait. *HMS Paragon* was hit by a torpedo, and although the crew continued to fight as the burning ship sank, 76 of the crew of 85 were killed. Herbert Webley was one, and he is remembered on Panel 24 of the Portsmouth Naval Memorial.

# GORDON WILSON

**Service Number:**
**Rank:** Second-Lieutenant
Royal Flying Corps
**Born:** 1897
**Died:** 12th February 1917
**Buried:** Upavon Cemetery

Gordon Ivor Wilson was born in 1897 to Alexander and Amy Wilson in East Keal, Lincolnshire. By the 1911 Census, fourteen year-old Gordon was a boarder at Repton Public School in Derbyshire, and the family were now living at Shovel House in North Petherton.

In March 1915, Gordon gained his commission to the Yeomanry, attached to the Royal Flying Corps. A competent pilot with 30 hours solo flying behind him, he was sadly killed on Monday 12 February 1917.

Whilst flying at an altitude of about 600 feet, Gordon collided with another aircraft, piloted by Second Lieutenant George Trevor Brown, of the Wilts Regiment, also attached to the Royal Flying Corps. The machines crashed to the ground and both pilots were instantly killed. An inquest was held at the Hospital of the Central Flying School, concluding that both deaths were a tragic accident, as both aircraft were in good working order; both pilots were competent; and weather was not a factor.

Listed as 'George' on the North Petherton War Memorial, Gordon was buried at Plot 8 at the Upavon Cemetery.

### James Baker

Born in 1884 in Devon, James married Clara Pike and lived in Tappers Lane, North Petherton. He served with the Devonshire's during the war, but was wounded in April 1918, returned home in May 1918 and was discharged on 05 August 1918 - he had suffered perforating shell wounds to his chest and abdomen. He died on 27 September 1919 at the age of 35 and is buried in North Petherton Cemetery.

### Horatious Chidgey

Born in 1886, Horatious married Alice Horner and lived in the town. Having served before the war, he was remobilised in August 1914 as part of the 5th Field Ambulance. Horatious died in 1927.

### Albert George Harris

Born in 1894, Albert joined the Somerset Light Infantry at the outbreak of the war, but was killed on 26 August 1914 and was buried in Nord Fontaine-au-Pire Communal Cemetery. At the time of his death his parents were living in Queen Street in North Petherton, but his name appears on the memorial at Norton Fitzwarren - where they had lived for most of Albert's life.

### Francis Rich

Born in 1896, both of his parents came from North Petherton, and by 1911 he was living in Southgate Avenue, Bridgwater. He enlisted with the 20th Territorial Force Depot, Royal Engineers and died at South Stoneham in Hampshire. Francis was buried at Heathfield Cemetery, Old Road in North Petherton.

# RICHARD BAKER

**Service Number:** 5577275
**Rank:** Private
Wiltshire Regiment
**Born:** 11 October 1922
**Died:** 25 August 1943
**Buried:** North Petherton Cemetery

Richard John Baker was born on 11 October 1922 to James and Ethel Baker, who lived in North Petherton. After attending North Petherton school, Richard got a job as a gardener and lived with the family he was working for in Bridgwater.

During the Second World War, Richard joined the Wiltshire Regiment, who were raising an additional two battalions to join its two regular army battalions. Sadly, Richard was killed during a exercise that was part of his initial training on 25 August 1943. As a result, his body was returned home and is buried at Section 3, Grave 3817 at North Petherton Cemetery.

*St Mary's Church, North Petherton*

# ALFRED BOND

**Service Number:** D/MX80266
**Rank:** Cook
     HMS Exeter
**Born:** 18 June 1916
**Died:** 28 February 1945
**Buried:** Ambon War Cemetery

Alfred John Bond was born on 18 June 1916 to Frederick and Emily Bond. After leaving North Petherton School, Alfred worked as a baker and confectioner in the White Hart Hotel, Wellington.

During the Second World War, Alfred's culinary skills were put to good use as he became a cook on board the heavy cruiser, HMS Exeter. During the Second Battle of the Java Sea, Japanese destroyers struck HMS Exeter with 18 torpedoes on 01 March 1942, sinking the ship and killing 40 of the crew. The Japanese rescued 652 men from the sea, Alfred included, and they were transferred to Macassar Prisoner of War Camp, Celebes. 152 of these rescued men died in Japanese captivity.

*HMS Exeter*

Alfred was one. He suffered from Pellagra (a lack of Vitamin B) and is buried at plot 29. B. 5. of the Ambon War Cemetery, Indonesia.

# ROBERT BOWRING

**Service Number:** 1333462
**Rank:** Sergeant
       35 Squadron
       RAF Volunteer Reserve
**Born:** 1923
**Died:** 04 July 1943
**Buried:** Heverlee War Cemetery,
       Belgium

Robert Abner Hugh Bowring  was born in 1923 in Bridgwater. His family later moved to North Petherton and Robert joined the Royal Air Force Volunteer Reserve.

He trained as an air gunner and joined 35 Squadron at its new base at RAF Boscombe Down, Wiltshire on 05 November 1940. Designated as the first Handley Page Halifax squadron, they soon moved to RAF Leeming, and then  to RAF Linton-on-Ouse, both in Yorkshire, by the end of the year. The squadron flew night bombing raids against targets in France and Germany throughout 1941 and into 1942.

*Handley Page Halifax Mark II*

The Handley Page Halifax Mark II was a four-engine heavy bomber that had a bomb capacity of over 6,000 Kg and a crew of seven.

In the summer of 1942 the squadron relocated to RAF Graveley, Cambridgeshire and continued with its almost nightly air raids on strategic targets on mainland Europe. On 03 July 1943, Robert's aircraft took off from RAF Graveley for the German city of Cologne. It was not heard from again. A German night fighter intercepted their Halifax and shot it down over the Netherlands, with the aircraft crashing near the town of Riemst, a few miles from Maastricht. The Air Ministry reported the crew as missing, presumed Killed in Action.

After the war, there was a search for the crew and they were found at St Trond. Their remains were exhumed, identified and reinterred in Haverlee War Cemetery in 1947, with Robert Bowring being buried at plot 5. A. 3.

*Heverlee War Cemetery, Belgium*

# FREDERICK BROOKS

**Service Number:** 14708606
**Rank:** Private
4th Battalion
Somerset Light Infantry
**Born:** 07 January 1926
**Died:** 07 March 1945
**Buried:** Reichswald Forest War
Cemetery, Germany

Frederick Joseph Brooks was born on 07 January 1926 to Charles and Anne Brooks in North Petherton. He attended North Petherton School and was still at school when the Second World War broke out in 1939.

He signed up just as soon as he could in Taunton, and joined the 4th Battalion of the Somerset Light Infantry. The 4th Battalion took part in the campaign for North-West Europe as part of the 43rd Wessex Division and Frederick joined up with them as soon as his basic training was complete in early 1945.

*Reichswald Forest War Cemetery, Germany*

He was immediately thrown into Operation Veritable, also known as the Battle of the Reichswald, alongside the First Canadian Army, between 08 February and 11 March 1945.

The fighting was hard as the 4th Battalion moved through the Netherlands and into the northern part of the Reichswald. Once they had advanced through the forest, they looked to take the towns of Rees, Kleve and Goch.

Frederick Brooks was killed on 07 March 1945 and is buried at plot 57. E. 19. of the Reichswald Forest War Cemetery - located in the German town of Kleve, close to the Dutch border.

*Reichswald Forest War Cemetery, Germany*

# HENRY ECKLEY

**Service Number:** 5671394
**Rank:** Corporal
      7th Battalion
      Somerset Light Infantry
**Born:** October 1917
**Died:** 09 August 1944
**Buried:** Tilly-Sur-Seulles War
      Cemetery, France

Henry George Eckley was born in October 1917 to George and Edith Eckley in North Petherton.

He signed up to the 7th Battalion, Somerset Light Infantry and then married his childhood sweetheart, Ruby Hill, in January 1940 in Bridgwater. After his initial training, Henry joined up with the 7th Battalion as they prepared to take part in Operation Overlord. Although not crossing the English Channel on D-Day itself, Henry and the rest of the 7th Battalion, landed on the beach at Courseulles-Sur-Mer in Normandy (better known as *Juno* beach) on 22 June 1944.

*Courseulles-Sur-Mer, Normandy*

After landing, the 7th Battalion initially headed to the outskirts of Caen, before becoming part of Operation Bluecoat - an allied attack with the aim of securing the road junction of Vire and the high ground of Mont Pinçon (the highest point of the Calvados region of Normandy). It was here, on Mont Pinçon, that Corporal Eckley was wounded and later died on 09 August 1944. He was 26 years old. Henry Eckley was buried at plot II. B. 10. at the Tilly-Sur-Seulles War Cemetery.

*Memorial on the top of Mont Pinçon*

*Tilly-Sur-Seulles War Cemetery, Normandy*

# JAMES GREEN

**Service Number:** 2072910
**Rank:** Sapper
   81 Assault Squadron
   Royal Engineers
**Born:** April 1920
**Died:** 01 October 1944
**Buried:** Calais Canadian War
   Cemetery

James Albert Green was born in April 1920 to Henry and Sarah Green, who lived in North Petherton. He signed up at the outbreak of the Second World War, joining the Royal Engineers as a Sapper. The Royal Engineers provided engineering and technical support that essentially made sure the troops kept moving.

Calais was liberated in September 1944, and as the allies advanced into Belgium in pursuit of retreating German forces, James was killed on 01 October 1944. He was buried at plot 3. A. 9 of the Calais Canadian War Cemetery in Leubringhen - a village halfway between Calais and Boulogne.

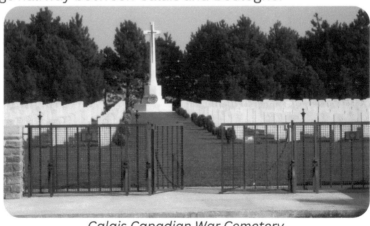

*Calais Canadian War Cemetery*

# THOMAS HADDON

**Service Number:** D/SSX 33733
**Rank:** Able Seaman
      HM Submarine H.44
**Born:** 26 February 1920
**Died:** 09 September 1941
**Commemorated:** Plymouth Naval
            Memorial

Thomas Robert George Haddon was born on 26 February 1920 to Mrs Alice Haddon (a widow) in North Petherton. Upon leaving school he worked as a printer's apprentice, before joining the Royal Navy at the outbreak of war.

*HM Submarine H. 44*

Thomas became one of 22 crew members on board HM Submarine H.44. Sadly, he was lost overboard at sea and was listed as missing, presumed killed, during naval exercises just off Campbeltown, Scotland on 09 September 1941.

He is remembered on Panel 47, Column 1 of the Plymouth Naval Memorial.

*Plymouth Naval Memorial*

# WILFRED HOOPER

**Service Number:** 5674382
**Rank:** Private
    1st Battalion
    Oxford & Bucks Light Infantry
**Born:** 1919
**Died:** 27 May 1940
**Buried:** Hazebrouck Communal
    Cemetery, France

Wilfred Walker Hooper was born in 1919 to Arthur and Emily Hooper of North Petherton. After attending school at North Petherton, he signed up to the Oxford & Bucks Light Infantry in 1939, relocating to France as part of the British Expedionary Force (BEF) in January 1940. When the BEF made its retreat towards Dunkirk, the 1st Battalion took part in the Battle of the Ypres-Comines Canal. Lasting a few days from 26-28 May 1940, they fought to keep this vital escape route towards Dunkirk open for as long as possible. It was during this battle, that Wilfred Hooper was killed on 27 May 1940. He was buried at Plot 4. Row C. Grave 1. of the Hazebrouck Communal Cemetery, south-east of Calais and Dunkirk.

*Hazebrouck Communal Cemetery*

# WILLIAM HUBBARD

**Service Number:** 5679507
**Rank:** Private
     10th Battalion
     Gloucestershire Regiment
**Born:** 17 July 1914
**Died:** 23 November 1944
**Buried:** Taukkyan War Cemetery,
     Myanmar

William Ernest Hubbard was born on 17 July 1914 to Abraham and Caroline Hubbard in North Petherton. After leaving school, William became a general labourer, but then joined the 10th Battalion of the Gloucestershire Regiment a little while after the Second World War broke out.

The 10th Battalion of the Glosters arrived on the Arakan Peninsula (modern day Rakhine) in February 1944 as part of the British effort in Burma (now Myanmar). The battalion moved to northern Burma and was engaged in four days of particularly fierce fighting at Pinwe in November. It was here, on 23 November 1944, that William was killed, and he was buried in plot 6. H. 19. of the Taukkyan War Cemetery.

*Taukkyan War Cemetery*

# RICHARD MARCHENT

**Service Number:** 14276992
**Rank:** Lance Corporal
2/5th Battalion
Leicestershire Regiment
**Born:** November 1923
**Died:** 14 September 1943
**Buried:** Salerno War Cemetery, Italy

Richard James Marchent was born in November 1923 to Charles and Elsie Marchent in North Petherton. He joined the army at the age of 18, in November 1942, and served with the 2/5th Battalion of the Leicestershire Regiment.

Since Dunkirk (May 1940) they had been stationed in England, but in January 1943 the Battalion took part in the 1st Army's landing in North Africa, and they suffered heavy casualties in and around Kassarine, a city in west-central Tunisia. Towards the end of August, they were preparing themselves to take part in Operation Avalanche - the Allied invasion of Italy.

*British troops landing on the beaches of Salerno*

On 09 September 1943, the allies, with a force of around 170,000 servicemen, landed near the vital port city of Salerno. A precursor to the D-Day landings in Normandy the following year, the British and American troops slowly established a beachhead.

A few days later, between 12–14 September, the German Army who were defending the area, launched some concerted counterattacks. The aim was to push the Salerno beachhead back into the sea before the other beachheads could link up with it. Heavy casualties were inflicted, as the Allied troops were spread too thinly, and Richard was one of them, being killed on 14 September 1943. He was just 19 years old.

Richard James Marchent was buried at plot IV. C. 39. of the Salerno War Cemetery in Italy. It is the final resting place of nearly 2,000 men and is just a few miles from the beaches many of them lost their lives on.

*Salerno War Cemetery, Italy*

# STANLEY POCOCK

**Service Number:** 5672998
**Rank:** Private
      7th Battalion
      Somerset Light Infantry
**Born:** October 1919
**Died:** 12 August 1944
**Buried:** Tilly-Sur-Seulles War
        Cemetery, France

Stanley Pocock was born in October 1919 to Fred and Minnie Pocock in Bridgwater.

In October 1941 he married Madge Peggy Roberts, moved to North Petherton and then signed up to the 7th Battalion, Somerset Light Infantry. After his initial training, Stanley joined up with the battalion as they prepared to take part in Operation Overlord. Although not crossing the English Channel on D-Day itself, Stanley and the rest of the 7th Battalion, landed on the beach at Courseulles-Sur-Mer in Normandy (better known as Juno beach) on 22 June 1944.

*Memorial in the small village of Cauville*

After landing, they became part of Operation Bluecoat - an allied attack with the aim of securing the road junction of Vire and the high ground of Mont Pinçon (the highest point of the Calvados region of Normandy).

After taking Mont Pinçon, the battalion headed across country and encountered a strong enemy position a few miles away at the small village of Cauville. It was here, on 12 August 1944, that Stanley was killed, aged just 24.

Stanley Pocock was buried at plot VII. E. 11. at the Tilly-Sur-Seulles War Cemetery in Normandy, along with over 1,000 other servicemen.

*Tilly-Sur-Seulles War Cemetery, Normandy*

# ARTHUR QUICK

**Service Number:** EC/10780
**Rank:** Lieutenant
      Indian Signal Corps
**Born:** 1919
**Died:** 22 November 1945
**Buried:** North Petherton Cemetery

Arthur George Quick was born in 1919 to Albert and Kate Quick of North Petherton. He joined the Indian Signal Corps and served in India throughout the Second World War. After coming home on leave for a few months after the war had finished, Arthur was heading back to India. On 22 November 1945, Arthur boarded a Consolidated Liberator, belonging to 53 Squadron RAF, which crashed shortly after take-off from RAF Merryfield in Somerset. The aircraft failed to gain height to clear a hill after take-off and struck a tree. It crashed at White's Farm near Broadway Pound, killing all 27 occupants. As this was close to his home town, Arthur was buried in Section 4 of North Petherton Cemetery.

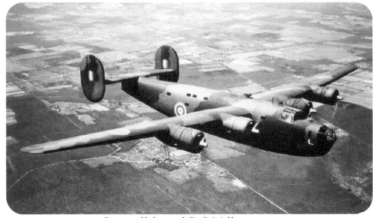

*Consolidated B-24 Liberator*

# ROBERT SMITH

**Service Number:** 5678444
**Rank:** Private
     10th Battalion
     Somerset Light Infantry
**Born:** 08 June 1913
**Died:** 01 May 1942
**Buried:** North Petherton Cemetery

Robert George Smith was born on 08 June 1913 to Robert and Kate Smith in North Petherton. After leaving school, Robert became a labourer and then signed up at Jellalabad Barracks in Taunton with the 10th Battalion of the Somerset Light Infantry, which was formed in 1940.

Robert was sadly killed on 01 May 1942 during a training exercise and was buried in Section 3 Grave 3808 at North Petherton Cemetery.

*Jellalabad Barracks, Taunton*

# RONALD WILLIAMS

**Service Number:** 5674450
**Rank:** Private
      1st Bucks Battalion
      Oxford & Bucks Light Infantry
**Born:** 03 October 1918
**Died:** 07 September 1943
**Buried:** Poznan Old Garrison
         Cemetery, Poland

Ronald Clifford Williams was born 03 October 1918 to Clifford and Florence Williams in North Petherton. In 1939, Ronald was a grocery shop assistant but soon joined the 1st Battalion, Oxford & Bucks Light Infantry, relocating to France as part of the British Expedionary Force (BEF) in January 1940. When the BEF made its retreat towards Dunkirk, the 1st Battalion fought a rear-guard action in the Battle of the Ypres-Comines Canal. Ronald was captured and subsequently held at Stalag XXI-D, a German prisoner-of-war camp based in Poznań, Poland. He died here on 07 September 1943, and after the war was buried at plot 8. B. 6. of the Poznań Old Garrison Cemetery.

*Poznan Old Garrison Cemetery, Poland*

*Official opening of Memorial Playing Field, July 1960*

*The dedication stone, November 2020*

*Memorial Park benefitted from significant investment in 2021*

In 1960, after fifteen years of planning and raising money, the Parish Council finally purchased a substantial plot of land on the corner of Taunton Road and Newton Road from local land owner Frank Harding. It was to be a permanent playing field in commemoration of those local servicemen and women who lost their lives as a result of the Second World War.

# NORTH PETHERTON REMEMBERS

In researching and creating this book, it was important to involve the local community as much as possible - and the Year 6 children at North Petherton Community Primary School embarked on a *North Petherton Remembers Project* in the autumn of 2022.

*Year 6 biographies*

*One of the pupils got to meet the granddaughter of the man she was writing about!*

*Remembrance Walk at the school*

The pupils received the background research that would later be used for creating this book, and then used their writing skills to create biographies of the 55 men on the town's war memorial, as well as producing some rather poignant artwork.

These were put on public display along a *Remembrance Walk* from the school to the church, and were up for the duration of the 2022 Remembrance weekend. The children also planned and led the Remembrance service at St Mary's Church, at 11am on 11 November 2022.

*Pupils sharing their biographies in the church service*

*Remembrance Walk*

A large number of parents and members of the community attended the church service and then explored the Remembrance Walk around the village. The children showed great maturity, empathy and understanding throughout the project.

North Petherton will remember.

*Remembrance Walk*

*With thanks to North Petherton Community School:*
Brinsley Baker, Heidi Baxter, Ashton Beecher, Morgan Blake, Jack Bunce, Eleanor Caddy, Tommy Carter, Amy Chown, Enzo Cinicola, Luca Cinicola, Edith Crocker, Lillyana Curry, Elli Ennis, Hannah Eva, Zack Evans, Lulu Godfrey, Samuel Harding, Amelia Harriott, Beren Hector, Evie Hetherington, Archie Hughes, Finley Humphrys, Noah Langdon, Madeline Mills, Amy Mitchell, Arran Murray-Smith, Ruben Pendlebury, Ella-Louise Potter, Lucas Puddy, Amiee Purchase, Elsie Rogers, Arthur Sanders, Michael Searle, Katie Selby, Zoe Semken, Jenson Sims, Hollie Stalley, Jessica Stenning, Harvey Thompson, Alexis Topley-Bird, Charlie Tutt, Emma Valentine, Tyler W-Perkins, Ava Williams, Beau Williams, India Williams, Maici-Lily Woodland, Tobias Wootton, Louis Wright, Zac Wright, Mia Wyatt, Maria Benjafield, Callum White and Sarah Penfold.

# ACKNOWLEDGEMENTS

There are a number of people who need thanking for their help in making this project become a reality.

Tony Emptage for his hard work in locating the grave photographs.
Jane Haslam & Wendy Taylor-Tancock for sharing their research on the names from the Great War; Nele Bille from the Commonwealth War Graves Commission in sourcing photographs of each cemetery; Sam Mundell for helping to research the Second World War names; Sarah Nathaniel, Jon Wort, John Harris and Peter King for sharing photographs; All at North Petherton Community Primary School for their support and enthusiasm for the project, especially Maria Benjafield, Callum White and Sarah Penfold - and of course the year 6 cohort who took great pride in honouring the men of North Petherton.

**Photograph credits:**

Front Cover (Clockwise from top left) Laurin Espie, Andrew Powell-Thomas, Margaret Pocock, Sabine Leclercq; Page 6 Peter King; Page 7 Andrew Powell-Thomas; Page 8 Janice Dennis, Public Domain; Page 9 Mick McCann, Dirk Debleu; Page 10 CWGC; Page 11 Public Domain, CWGC, N Norma; Page 12 Laurin Espie; Page 13 Dirk Debleu, A Len; Page 14 Nader Habash; Page 15 A Andrew, Hagai Agmon-Snir; Page 16 Andrew Powell-Thomas; Page 17 Regis Biaux, CWGC; Page 18 Chris & Jean Cosgrove, CWGC; Page 19 Bob Pike, CWGC; Page 20 CWGC, CWGC, Battle of Loos; Page 21 CWGC, CWGC, Tony Donnelly; Page 22 Senthil Nathan; Page 23 Partho Burman; Page 24 Sabine Leclercq, CWGC; Page 25 CWGC, Julie & David Thompson; Page 26 CWGC; Page 27 CWGC, Nader Habash; Page 28 Johan de Jonghe, Sam Mundell; Page 29 Sam Mundell, Johan de Jonghe; Page 30 Ibrahim Jaradah, Andrew Powell-Thomas; Page 31 CWGC, CWGC; Page 32 Barry Gage, CWGC; Page 33 CWGC, Mick McCann; Page 34 A Other, CWGC; Page 35 Public Domain, Mick McCann; Page 36 Nancy Wright, Public Domain; Page 37 CWGC, Andrew Powell-Thomas; Page 38 Diaa Omara, CWGC; Page 39 Dirk Debleu, Sabine Declerq; Page 40 CWGC, Julie & David Thompson; Page 41 Eleni Kakkava, CWGC; Page 42 Carol Constable, Public Domain; Page 43 CWGC, Kenneth Celie; Page 44 Archie Needs, CWGC; Page 45 CWGC, Valerie Habracken; Page 46 Mick McCann, Public Domain; Page 47 A Freedman; Page 48 S Sister, CWGC; Page 49 CWGC, J Jamison, CWGC; Page 50 Public Domain, Public Domain; Page 51 SLMGC, CWGC; Page 52 Public Domain, Public Domain; Page 53 Blueheaven, John Harris; Page 54 Tony Emptage, Dirk Debleu; Page 55 CWGC, Mick McCann, CWGC; Page 56 Michel, CWGC; Page 57 CWGC, CWGC; Page 58 Sarah Nathaniel, Public Domain, Brad Evans; Page 59 Mick McCann, CWGC; Page 60 Nancy Wright, John Lakeland; Page 61 Sabine Declercq, CWGC; Page 62 Public Domain, Public Domain; Page 63 Public Domain, Sarah Nathaniel, Keith Roberts; Page 64 Jon Wort; Page 66 Janice Dennis, Andrew Powell-Thomas; Page 67 Jenny Ashcraft, Public Domain; Page 68 Pierre Vandervelden, Public Domain; Page 69 CWGC; Page 70 Ivor C Brooks, CWGC; Page 71 Des Phillipet, CWGC; Page 72 Andrew Powell-Thomas (2); Page 73 Andrew Powell-Thomas (2); Page 74 M Len, CWGC; Page 75 CWGC, Kevin Blair, Cliff Barry; Page 76 Valerie Habracken, CWGC; Page 77 Tony Buckley, CWGC; Page 78 Nele Bille, Public Domain; Page 79 CWGC; Page 80 Margaret Pocock, Andrew Powell-Thomas; Page 81 Andrew Powell-Thomas (2); Page 82 Taylor McLean, Public Domain; Page 83 Janice Dennis, Andrew Powell-Thomas; Page 84 M Paul, CWGC; Page 85 Peter King, Andrew Powell-Thomas (2); Page 86 Andrew Powell-Thomas (3); Page 87 North Petherton Community School (5), Andrew Powell-Thomas (2)